Swire Smith

Educational comparisons or Remarks on industrial schools in England, Germany and Switzerland

Swire Smith

Educational comparisons or Remarks on industrial schools in England, Germany and Switzerland

ISBN/EAN: 9783337198176

Printed in Europe, USA, Canada, Australia, Japan

Cover: Foto ©Paul-Georg Meister /pixelio.de

More available books at **www.hansebooks.com**

EDUCATIONAL COMPARISONS

OR

Remarks on Industrial Schools in England

Germany and Switzerland

BY

SWIRE SMITH

Hon. Sec. to Trade School Council and Mechanics' Institute
Keighley

LONDON: SIMPKIN, MARSHALL, & CO
BRADFORD: T. BREAR
KEIGHLEY: J. L. CRABTREE

1873

PRICE SIXPENCE

The statements regarding Education in Germany and Switzerland contained in this pamphlet are mainly based upon facts collected during two visits to the Continent in 1872. The substance of the following pages was delivered as a Lecture in the Mechanics' Institute, Keighley, on January 1st, 1873, ISAAC HOLDEN, Esq., in the Chair. It is now printed, at the request of the meeting, with some alterations and additions.

EDUCATIONAL COMPARISONS.

THE manufacturing town of Keighley is representative in many respects of a number of towns in the country which are rapidly rising in wealth, population and influence. Its staple industries are—the spinning of worsted yarns, the weaving of mixed fabrics, and the making of machinery and tools of various kinds. These, and such industries as the building trades, which flourish side by side with them, give employment to nearly the whole of the population, and the demand for labour extends not more to the able-bodied men than to the women and children. In consequence of the compulsory powers of the Factory Acts, it may be said that a great proportion of the present generation of the inhabitants has enjoyed the advantage of an attendance at school, at least between the ages of eight and thirteen. We may, therefore, anticipate that the elementary instruction of the people of this town will be found, on examination, to be more general and effective than in most English towns of the same size, but dependent upon different industries. Perhaps the local conditions may be expected to prove less favourable to the higher education given in good English Secondary Schools.

As an evidence of the general intelligence of the town, the Mechanics' Institute and Schools of Science and Art are, perhaps, not surpassed by any in the country in the facilities which they offer by evening classes and other means for systematically carrying forward, and directing into useful channels, the education received in the Day Schools. It is

B

encouraging to state that these facilities are largely taken advantage of. The town has reaped its fair share of the material prosperity of the country during the last thirty years, and in frugality it is probably ahead of most of its neighbours. The criminal offences are neither so numerous nor so grave as in many other towns of equal population; and, judging from the number of religious edifices, their handsome construction, their tasteful arrangement, and, above all, from the number and excellence of the Sunday Schools, Keighley may fairly take credit for marching abreast of the times in the progress of civilisation.

I propose to bring before your notice a few facts in relation to the actual educational position of Keighley as it presents itself to a citizen of the town interested in its welfare. I shall also give some impressions respecting the education of similar towns in some other countries. In doing so, I desire, in the course of this paper, to draw your attention to the following topics :—

1. The education and industrial training which the boys and girls of England (and more particularly of Keighley) receive at present (and have received during the past few years) in elementary and secondary schools.

2. The education which boys and girls of a similar position in life are receiving in Germany and Switzerland.

3. How the education of the boys and girls of Keighley may be made more systematic, comprehensive, and general.

I shall not have much to say of the higher branches of literary education, but in reference to the other branches I shall assume that any suggestions which apply to Keighley as an industrial manufacturing town with its 25,000 to 30,000 inhabitants, would apply with equal force to any or all such towns in the kingdom.

I will endeavour, then, in the first place, to describe in a simple manner the actual education which boys and girls receive in Keighley, as a preparation for the duties of life. As you are aware, before certain School Boards took advantage of the compulsory powers given them under the Education Act of 1870, education in England had not been compulsory, except so far as it related to children employed in factories* and workshops. In their case half-time attendance was and is enforced between the ages of eight and thirteen. As to children not thus employed, there had been no compulsion whatever; so that in the rural districts surrounding us, and in nearly all the agricultural counties—where the Factory Acts are not in force—the education given is still deplorable in the extreme; so much so that it is said that a great proportion of the children start out in life unable to read or write. We will hope that this cannot be said to so great an extent of the children of Keighley. I am aware that there are great numbers who never enter a school until they commence at the age of eight to work at the factory; but, as a rule, the Keighley boy, at the age of five or six, is sent to a private dame school, or to one of the infant schools in connection with the several primary denominational schools of the town. Of these there are some half-dozen comparatively large establishments,† used as day and Sunday schools, and conducted by the Church of England, the Wesleyans, and Roman Catholics. They are attended by the children of the labouring population, nearly all of whom, after the age of eight, become half-timers, while very few indeed remain after the age of thirteen. The schools are

* Not more than 50,000 children are employed in factories.
† National School, St. Mary's, St. John's, Wesleyan, Wesley Place, Catholic.

under Government Inspection, and grants are made by the Education Department on the results of their teaching and on the attendance of pupils. Secondary education has been given in a few private schools, not assisted or inspected by Government, and since the reorganisation of the Grammar School (the premises of which are now a girls' school) it has been offered to boys of all classes in the Trade School of the Mechanics' Institute, in connection with the Science and Art Department, South Kensington. The sons and daughters of some of the wealthier inhabitants are sent to boarding schools, and there are a few isolated instances of youths who are completing their education on the Continent or at the Universities.

Such is the present provision for the education of the boys and girls of Keighley; and by those good people who don't care to look below the surface it will probably be considered satisfactory. For I have noticed generally, that the fact of there being in any town a certain number of schools with a given amount of so called "sufficient accommodation" for the number attending, is accepted by most people as a guarantee that the instruction imparted is fully up to the requirements also, without considering that it is quite possible to be attending school and not learning, over-looking too the important fact that although the door may be open there are many neglected children who never go in, but receive as their only teaching the pernicious education of the street and the gutter.

To inquire more closely, the boy who attends the primary school commences—as I have said before—his serious education at eight, and continues it during half the day until he is thirteen. During this time he is taught in a room which is often ill furnished, ill lighted, and worse ventilated, but almost invariably crowded with children; sometimes to the number of from 200 to 300 in one room. He is generally under the direction of pupil teachers of more or less capacity and experience, but now and then receives a lesson from the certificated master. The din of the school-room may often be heard far beyond its outer walls ; disturbances are constantly arising which cause an uproar in the whole assembly, until the confusion and noise render it simply impossible for the teacher to fix and command the attention of the pupils, and one cannot but marvel how, under such circumstances, any effective educational training can be gone through, or any substantial progress made. In some English schools— and I would fain hope that this cannot be said of Keighley —the teaching is so devoid of all system or of all means to rouse the mental faculties of the children, that intelligence is crushed, and a hatred of all study arises. An Inspector of Schools, in describing this deplorable want of interest, declared that " in certain schools he could tell pretty accurately, by the pupils' faces, how long they had been at school. The longer the period, the more stupid, vacant, and expressionless the face." Another School Inspector, illustrating the same state of things, when examining a class in The Acts of the Apostles, asked—" Why did the eunuch go away rejoicing?" The answer frankly was—" Please sir, because Philip had a done o' teaching on him !" I will leave you to judge " what hours of weariness and waste are summed up in this brief story ! Such teaching defeats its own end; the power to read is gained at the cost of the desire to read."* The boys are expected to advance a standard each year, and the " highest standard," upon which the energies of the teaching

* Paper by Dr. W. B. Hodgson. Social Science Meeting, Belfast, Sept., 1867.

staff were directed, previous to the Code of 1871, simply required reading a short ordinary paragraph in a newspaper, or other modern narrative, writing from dictation from a similar source, and in arithmetic, a sum in practice, or bills of parcels. In the present Code, however (1872), the standards are raised, and the sixth requires ability to read " with fluency and expression," to write "a short theme, or letter, or an easy paraphrase," and to work a sum in " proportion and vulgar or decimal fractions." As a rule, the elements of the sciences are not taught, but in some schools, religion, geography, history, and drawing are taught a little. The same course is gone through by the girls, with the addition of a little plain needlework, but since they are often required as helps in the family during their school age, and since the British public still holds the absurd belief that the education of girls is not a matter of consequence—the schooling which they receive is often of a still more limited character. I have heard in Keighley of classes taught in the outer porch of the school because of the great crowd within, and I have seen a class assembled in the playground in order to escape the vitiated air and the Babel-like noise which I could hear going on inside. The head teacher of an elementary school in Keighley told me not long ago that many children come to school at ten or eleven who do not know their letters, and many leave at the age of thirteen unable to read or write. The difficulty constantly to be contended against is the evasion of the law on the part of many of the parents, whose main object seems to be, not to get their children educated, but to have them passed full time at the factory, and who resort to most disgraceful deceptions in order to attain this object. In this the parents are too often supported by the children, some of whom look upon the teaching which they have received as a drudgery which they are delighted to escape, and cannot be prevailed upon to continue their schooling beyond the minimum fixed by the law. You may think that I overstate the case, for all of you will be able to point to instances of boys and girls who do not look upon learning in the light I have described, and are further advanced in their studies than my statements would lead you to infer. I doubt not that many of you believe that *all* boys and girls who go through the schools actually learn at least to read, write and cypher. Yet let us see what official figures say. I· find from the Education Report of 1871-72 that there were during the last year 1,231,434 children in average attendance at the Government Elementary Day Schools of England and Wales. Excluding infants, there were nearly a million, of whom more than 300,000 were over ten years of age, but of the whole million only 29,053 were presented for examination in the sixth standard. Of these but 19,735 passed in the three subjects, not 2 per school, and less than 2 per cent. of the total pupils. Figures such as these speak very discouragingly of the educational condition of the nation; and it is quite beyond my power to give you an adequate impression of what they really mean. From the fact that one-third of the work of the year was tested by a higher standard renders it difficult to ascertain, with any degree of accuracy, the attainments of the pupils, but I find, in going back to the examinations of 1870, contained in the previous year's report, that, from an average attendance of 1,152,389, less than 23,000 passed in the three subjects of the sixth standard, or but one-half per cent. more than passed under the raised standard of 1871; in other words, less than $2\frac{1}{2}$ per 100 of all the children attending our Elementary Day Schools a year ago (excluding infants) were proved to possess a fair knowledge of reading, writing and arithmetic, and the moment the standard is raised the number of passes proportionately declines. Regarding the Keighley Schools, let us see what information we can gather from such statistics as I have been able to procure. Of the children who attended the Elementary Schools of the Keighley district* last year (including Oakworth), 1900 were qualified for examination, of whom 1580 were presented. Of these Mr. Baily, the District Inspector, who has kindly furnished me with statistics, says: " That about 900 children were over nine years old, presented in Standards I. and II." I have every reason for believing that if there is no public interference with the elementary education of Keighley it will continue, broadly speaking, to be administered in the future under the system which prevailed during the past year, and we may naturally look forward to results of a similar character. Assuming that such will be the case, I find from certain minutes in the New Code (1872),† that " after the 31st of March next no day scholar above nine years of age will be examined in Standard I.," and "after the 31st of March, 1874, no day scholar above nine years of age will be examined in Standard II." This really means that if we follow the system of the past a little over a year longer, under the same conditions of material and attendance, positively more than half of the children presented (57 per cent.) will be disqualified from earning any examination grants whatever. If these minutes had been in operation during the past year 900 children in the

---

* The Schools supplying accommodation recognised as efficient, are Keighley National; Keighley, Wesleyan; Keighley, Roman Catholic; Oakworth, National; Oakworth, Wesleyan (and Infants); Eastwood, National ; Ingrow, National; part of Wesley Place, Wesleyan (in Bingley district).

† Education Report, 1871-72. New Code p. lxxxiii.

Keighley district would probably not have been brought before the Inspector for examination at all, and the number would have been reduced from 1900 (who were qualified by age and attendance) to 680, who would have been actually presented. These figures commend themselves to our serious consideration; but it will be a matter of greater interest to you to know that in the fifth and sixth standards together, Mr. Baily believes that "less than 60 were examined," and but 40 out of the 1900 in all the standards were considered to possess any knowledge of geography, the only extra subject. I have not been able to ascertain the exact number of pupils who passed the sixth standard separately, but, supposing that half of those presented were found to possess a good knowledge of reading, writing and arithmetic—say 30, or less than 2 per cent. of the whole—I think, even then, we should not consider that we had much cause for boasting. The most important point, however, in this branch of our inquiry— What is the proficiency of the pupils when they leave the Day School altogether? — is one upon which there are no statistics to guide us.. I have, however, made careful estimates, and, with a sincere desire to treat the matter fairly and to err on the side of leniency, if at all, I am forced to the conclusion—which I now give to you as an opinion—that of of all the boys and girls who pass through our district Elementary Schools, not more than 15 per 100 receive a sound knowledge of reading, writing and arithmetic. And yet, forsooth, we repeatedly hear the statement that the Keighley Schools are giving an "efficient education." It is unnecessary for me to trouble you with figures respecting the actual acquirements of the backward pupils —the 60, 70, or 80 per cent. of all who. go through our national elementary schools, but I can speak with greater authority of the attainments of the best of them, for it has been my good fortune now for two years to see the work of the picked boys from the elementary schools in Keighley tested by examination. You will remember that the Council of the Trade School, anticipating the Scholarships of the Grammar School, have for two years offered free places (in the Trade School) to such boys of the artisan class from the elementary and other schools in the town, as should pass highest in a prescribed examination. The masters of the principal elementary schools have readily taken advantage of this offer, and, at the last examination, papers. were worked by seventeen boys, who, for natural aptitude, perseverance and attainments, may be fairly considered as standing at the head of all the boys in the town of the same age, numbering probably not less than 300, who have only the same opportunities of learning. Yet, if you were to see these papers, you would pronounce them, almost without exception, to be extremely unsatisfactory; and were it not that I should have been taking an unfair liberty, or that I might throw discouragement upon these excellent competitions in future, I should have asked permission of the Council to give illustrations from the papers themselves, which would have fully substantiated this criticism. Far be it from me to appear to attempt in the slightest degree to diminish the credit due to these worthy lads or their masters; relatively the honour due to them is all the same—for they were highest amongst so many—but this illustration reveals conclusively the faults of the system upon which our schools are managed. If the sharpest, brightest, and best trained lads in the elementary schools of Keighley—schools, mind you, which compare well with schools all over the country— are proved to be deficient in primary instruction, what are we to expect from the general average of boys whose attainments fall immeasurably below those of whose productions I have just spoken? It is idle to speak of these boys as being less talented than those of a higher sphere in life; it is from such ranks that some of the best men in every town and nation spring—no town has been more fruitful in them than Keighley—and in the Trade School at present, where the son of the artisan sits on the same bench as the son of his master, the faculty of learning is not possessed in a higher degree by the latter than by the former. I saw a statement the other day, upon the authority of an eminent School Inspector,* that six years of continuous and regular instruction are required to give a fair primary education, say from six years of age to twelve, and yet we in Keighley, in every elementary school in the town, are practically attempting to do the same thing in two-and-a-half or three years under our factory system, the masters being weighted at the same time with all kinds of difficulties and drawbacks. It stands to reason that if a boy only goes to school half day, he ought to have the advantage of considerably more than ordinary teaching power, if anything like justice is to be done to him—and especially may this be said of the somewhat jaded half-timers who attend in the afternoon. I am sure that the schoolmasters will bear me out in the opinion that instead of being overtaxed, as at present, they should be able to bring to bear upon their work at all times, intellects and energies fresh and vigorous, so as to enable them to give not the dry bones only, but the flesh and blood of the instruction which they are called upon to impart. It is unnecessary for me to speak at greater length of the

---

* D. R. Iearon, vol. vi., page 7, Schools Inquiry Commission.

primary national schools. A glance at any of the education reports will show that they are far from being up to the mark. Mr. Lowe, when he presided over the Education Department, calculated that " of the children that are in the schools which the grants of the Privy Council are intended to assist, *only one-ninth got the benefit of a really good education,*"* and a Royal Commission† reported—the last which inquired into this question—that in addition to many appalling deficiencies, there would be "*at least* 100,000 *outdoor pauper children totally uneducated.*" Judging from the antecedents of these children, we may guess what sort of training most of them really get, although "*they are precisely the children for whom the State is responsible.*" We know too well what sort of men and women are developed out of this mob of neglected children. Ignorant, discontented and vicious they are of necessity — openly criminal they are in a thousand cases. They load our prisons, absorb in alms fifty times over the cost of starting them in honest ways, and spend all times of illness, idleness and old age in workhouse wards at the public expense. The Commissioners say, and with undoubted truth, that if we could withdraw these children "from the influences which now corrupt them, we should cut off the principal roots of pauperism and crime." But in spite of this great complaint against educational destitution and inefficient means, our primary schools form the best administered branch of our national School system. Whatever may be their faults, there is this to be said for them, that they consistently do what they can to teach reading, writing, and arithmetic, the groundwork of every educational superstructure. In a greater or less degree, the masters do

---

* Speech, Feb. 13, 1862, Hansard, p. 198. † 1861.

attempt to teach these to all, and, generally speaking, in as systematic a manner as is possible under the circumstances. The evidence collected shows that in a great number of private uninspected schools, in which however nearly one-third* of the children of England are educated, the education given is far worse than in the inspected schools to which I have directed your attention.

Whether public or private—above the primary schools,—education has been pronounced as little better than a chaos. The numerous unreformed grammar schools scattered about the country, and the still greater number of private adventure schools for the middle classes, professing to give a secondary education, have been proved to be, in too many instances, conducted without any pretence of a system, and with very "little adaptation of means to ends, because there has been no general agreement as to the ends to be attained." I am not going to find fault with the private schools of Keighley, or the boarding schools in the neighbourhood, some of which I know to have done very creditable work, but the success of these has been by no means uniform. Of the old grammar schools of the country one can speak more freely, inasmuch as they are now in a sense public schools, and official documents have been written concerning them. I willingly admit that amongst these there have been some marked successes, which have been described as "fitful and accidental, and achieved rather in spite of our public measures than by the help of them;" and these exceptional successes have hindered the reform of the rest, by bolstering up an antiquated system which was wasting some of the best educational resources of the country, and sending boys

---

* C. S. Parker, " Questions for a Reformed Parliament," page 133.

out into the world untrained for the work of civilization in which all are called upon to bear a part. Mr. Forster would deserve the gratitude of his country as a statesman even if the framing and passing of the Endowed Schools Act were the only measure of successful parliamentary legislation that he could lay claim to, for in that measure he established a principle of profound wisdom by making secondary education national, in the sense of opening a way by which the poorest might receive a training of the highest order, and the middle classes one of a character suited to the requirements of the scholars of the localities in which such schools were placed. I know that the Endowed Schools Commission has been freely criticised for the manner in which it is in some instances performing the duties imposed upon it; but let any one ponder over the reports of the Schools Enquiry Commission, see there what strange abuses had crept into the old schools, and he will no doubt rise from the task with a full conviction that it was really time that new life and vigour should be breathed into these ancient foundations that had decayed in everything save in the value of their endowments and the obstinacy of their mismanagement. As we in Keighley are enjoying the benefits of two small trusts of this character, and as an argument was put forward strongly at the time of their re-organisation that the Government had no right to interfere with them, and that the wills of the founders should be carried out in spirit and in letter, I hope I may be excused for dwelling upon this part of the subject a little longer than otherwise I should have done, just to show that not only had the "dead hand of the past" been already pushed aside in regard to many trusts, the intentions of which were useful, clear and practicable, but that it was simply impossible that the strange freaks which some men perpetrated in their wills in the semi-barbarous ages long passed should be allowed to be carried out under the influence of the civilization and enlightenment of modern times. There were some schools also that were doing practically nothing but wasting the endowments upon the masters who might be in office without giving any educational equivalent at all.

Allow me to give you a few instances bearing upon these points. The Grammar School at Boston has an income of £792 a-year. When the Commissioners made their report, the head-master was teaching three boarders and no others, the under-master attended when it suited his convenience to do so, and the usher was teaching an inferior village school.

Sedbergh, with an income of £610 a-year, had thirteen boys attending when Mr. Fitch visited it, and it appeared as if this number would be reduced; the school-rooms were in a shameful state, and the discipline of the scholars was bad also.

As the Keighley schools are now reorganised, we will forget the past, and say nothing about them.

In one report, I find an amusing story from the pen of Mr. Fearon.* "At a certain Grammar School which I visited, with an income, according to Parliamentary returns, of over £400 a-year, and annually increasing, I found *two masters*, with fixed salaries, and *one scholar*. Perhaps one of the most comical scenes ever witnessed in that county was the examination of that one solitary scholar by the venerable and learned head-master, the usher, and the assistant commissioner. He was a sickly boy, and very ignorant. Before leaving the place, I ventured, as a matter of curiosity, to ask the master

---

* Schools Inquiry Commission, vol. vi., page 17.

on what pension he would be willing to retire. "I don't want to retire at all," said he. "But," said I, "you have only one scholar!" To which he made the astounding reply, "And I don't want any more. Why should I? I am an old man. This is a good house and garden, and the place is better than a curacy. I will not retire if I can help it, and certainly not for less than the full salary. Why should I?"

At Netherby, the schoolmaster was evidently a practical man : he kept a flour and spinning mill at the same time, and doubtless had solved the technical education problem long before it engaged public attention, by making his pupils as useful in the mills as in the school-room.

One benevolent gentleman, named Antony Pinchbeck, (in 1665,) anxious to do a good turn to his namesakes through the long ages of posterity, founded a school at Butterwick, in Lincolnshire, to all children "of the name of Pinchbeck," and some others. The master was to be named Pinchbeck also, if possible, and "be able to teach Latin and Greek." One would have thought that the prospects of so cheap an education would have tempted the neighbouring population generally to adopt the favoured name of Pinchbeck; yet, with an income of £312 a-year, "the amount of classical knowledge imparted in it was represented by two boys learning the declensions."

With some the idea became so fixed that the endowment was left for their special use, irrespective of duties to be performed in connection with it, that they looked upon teaching as simply secondary and optional. Here is an instance :—

"The head-master of Kington grammar school told Mr. Bompas, that it was not worth his while to push the school, as with the endowment (about £200 a-year), and some other sources of income, he had enough to live on comfortably without troubling himself to do so."*

At Whitgift's Hospital, Croydon, "the late master had found no pupils attending the school when he came, and never had any at all during the thirty years that he was master."

In these "good old times," it seems evident that some were determined that the child should not bo spoilt by "sparing the rod." There were frequent injunctions in the wills of school founders that the pupils were to subscribe "pennies to buy rods." "At Guildford, in 1608, the rod and broom-money was fixed at 8d. yearly, which, considering the difference in the value of money between that time and this, and the cheapness of the articles used, indicates an amount of thrashing which is quite appalling."

I need not pile up examples to show you the administration of the so-called secondary education of the country. I might refer at length to the qualifications of masters, and show how appointments were made on almost any grounds but those all important ones—fitness and ability to teach. An instance is reported of an appointment having been given to a *very* deaf man, who had "previously conducted a private school and made himself useful to his fellow-townsmen as vestry clerk." It was feared that if a competent man were put into the school, this poor fellow's private school would be ruined, so the trustees determined to give him the vacant mastership.†

This case is by no means extraordinary, for, according to Mr. Richmond, who inspected the Endowed Schools of

---

* Report, vol. i., 225.

† See Mr. Giffard's Endowed Schools Report, vol. ii., p. 123.

c

Suffolk, "more than one-fourth of the Grammar Schools in the county were suffering from the bodily infirmities of the master."

But worse than these, Mr. E. C. Tufnell says, "It has frequently occurred to me to cause the dismissal of a master from a pauper school, on account of gross ignorance, or gross immorality. The useful power of the Poor-Law Board prevents such people being again appointed to pauper schools, but I have taken the pains to ascertain what has become of those masters, and I have generally found, that they have got places as ushers in schools for the middle and upper classes."*

So much then for the wasting of precious endowments and for the employment of incompetent teachers. And yet there are people who have protested against any interference with these abuses. In some instances the founders themselves— —men of a past age in feeling and character—evidently wished to perpetuate the sports and pastimes of their day— which doubtless they considered to be manly, but which we look upon as coarse and brutal. Imagine such a will as this being carried out in the nineteenth century? Sir Thomas Boteler's executors in 1526, ordered the master to take "three potation pennies" in the year, "for the which he shall make a drinking for all the said scholars," and at Shrovetide one "cock penny," out of which the master was to procure a cock, which he fastened by a string to a post, and fixed in a pit for the boys to pelt with sticks. If a boy hit the cock it became his, but if no boy hit it, the master took it for himself. Others went in for cock fighting. Thus the statutes of Hartlebury School expressly authorise the master "to have

---

* Vol. ii. Miscellaneous Papers, p. 65.

and use and take the profits of all cock fights and potations as are commonly used in schools."

The abuses and the modifications of them which still exist in Grammar Schools will soon happily become remembrances of the past, and I have quoted a sufficient number of them to show that if there is reason to be dissatisfied with the general state of primary schools and education, there is a still greater cause to be ashamed of a system of so-called secondary education, which countenanced such strange anomalies. The case is no better so far as it relates to girls' schools. Good ones there are, but in general we hear the same tale of incompetent teachers, misapplied endowments, and an injudicious school course. There is the additional grievance that in not a few cases the endowment of a girls' school has been unjustly made over to the managers of a boys' school. The ladies, however, are taking up this question in good earnest; and as the Endowed Schools' Commissioners are required by the Act of 1869 to extend to girls the benefits of endowments, and are taking active steps to carry that requirement into effect, we may expect that the advantage of any improvement which may shortly take place in secondary education will be shared by girls as well as boys.

This brings me back again to secondary education in Keighley, where the two schools, the Trade School and the Grammar School for girls, form the inauguration of the new order of things, to which I shall have occasion to refer presently.

At the age of thirteen nearly all the boys and girls attending the primary schools begin working full time, and their compulsory attendance at school ceases. Those of a higher social position, who are sent to private schools, continue usually for two or three years longer, while the very few who are being trained for the learned professions, or whose parents desire for them a superior education, for its own sake, "finish" at the universities, or at some of the public or private schools of the continent.

The boys find full field for their strength and energies in the various trades of the district, all ready to receive them, all offering valuable prizes for intelligence, skill and aptitude; of which the leaders are constantly looking out for those who are training heads and hands to steady application and faithful work. The practical discipline of the workshop and the factory takes the place, during the day, of the school,—it is a stern discipline to many, and sometimes developes noble qualities—but this is a critical period for all young men, for in their hours of leisure during the six or seven years that follow, those habits are formed which, for good or ill, ofttimes cling to them for a lifetime. After work hours, there is no restraint upon the young man but that of home, which, I am sorry to say, is not always well directed; he is probably one of the seven or eight boys out of every ten, unable at thirteen to read a newspaper fluently, or work a simple sum; he has left school and its drudgery; having learnt little, he doesn't value it; and his companions are no better instructed than he. It may thus be seen that this boy has spent educationally thirteen years of his life to very little purpose; his cheap education, without results, which has left his last state as bad as the first, has been most expensive to all who have had to pay for it. It has been so to his parents, for they have been deprived of years of labour, and years of school fees, at probably a pinching time; it has been so to the State, for it has been supplementing the fees of the parents by public taxes; but it is more expensive still to himself, because he has got no practical good out of it ; his precious morning hours have been wasted; and to the end he may go through the world undeveloped and unrefined, at the mercy of a thousand temptations that offer flattering baits, in order to lure him astray from the paths of virtue. How can any lover of his country be satisfied with such results ? What economy can there be in such a system? The soil, which with proper cultivation in its virgin freshness, might have been made capable of yielding fifty or a hundred-fold for all the labour expended upon it, is allowed to be become trodden as the mere way side, impenetrable to good seed, or neglected like the thorny ground, which chokes with its weeds and briars all the good seed that falls there.

Some boys and girls, however, even in the factory schools, have learned to use with proficiency and delight the tools with which they can dig knowledge for themselves; and these, by the start which they have made, and following up their opportunities by steady application, become the men and women who rise to positions of trust and responsibility, and merit the respect which on all hands is usually liberally accorded to them.

There are boys, too, among the neglected ones, who naturally lean to better things, who have the wisdom to see their shortcomings and the energy to attempt to overcome them. During their apprenticeship they awaken up to a knowledge of the difficulties that lie in the path of every man who has the world to grapple with, and they resolutely set to work by one method or another and seek an acquaintance with those arts and sciences that teach them to derive pleasure and profit from the sublime works of nature or the wonderful creations of the genius of man. Many of these two classes—so far as Keighley is concerned, perhaps nearly the whole of them—come to the evening classes of the Mechanics' Institute that they may improve themselves, and here I have had the opportunity of noticing the proficiency which they have attained when they commence their studies. These youths, bear in mind, are the most thoughtful, the most industrious and painstaking that are to be met with in this and in every town, and we are all proud of them; and yet,—I do not speak in any way disrespectfully of them—the masters complain that the attainments of many are of a very low order: I should be astonished were it otherwise. Apprentices come expecting to take up the sciences. Young joiners, masons, mechanics, and representatives of other trades, come, knowing that a knowledge of building construction, practical and theoretical mechanics, and other subjects treating of the strength of materials, the erection of buildings, and the making of machinery, would be of great advantage to them. They find, to their bitter disappointment, when they really have to face their work, that they have come to learn mathematics, knowing next to nothing of arithmetic; that their spelling is so bad that some of them cannot write out the problems dictated to them by the master. Throughout all the sciences, from chemistry downwards, and to a great extent in the case of drawing also,—which has been pronounced "the main spring of a technical education,"*— the same difficulty of want of foundation and groundwork is experienced.† And the obstacles that have to be overcome

---

* Professor Jenkin.

† In view of the demand now so loudly made for workmen of higher technical skill, it is melancholy to report that nearly 90 per cent. of our present scholars leave the primary schools, not only uninstructed in the elements of science, but also destitute of the rudimentary knowledge without which all future teaching of science, even if it were offered to them, would be well-nigh unintelligible.—Mr. Fitch's Report, 1867.

are such as quell many a stout heart. Ask a novice who
has passed the age of boyhood to imitate on the ice the
graceful evolutions of the practised skater; fasten a pair
of skates to his feet and set him off! What is the result?
Hard knocks, bruised shins and elbows, a ridiculous
awkwardness, and, ten to one, a determination on his part
never to try the ice again. But yet the would-be skater
has much in his favour compared with the would-be
scholar; the pastime is delightful, it is an exhilarating
and healthy exercise, and generally gives him the benefit
of cheerful company in inclement weather. The student at
the night class has none of these advantages. He leaves
his comfortable fireside, somewhat wearied with the physical
toil of the day; his difficulties are greater than those of
the skater; his humiliation at his awkwardness is more
keen and painful, yet manfully he encounters the drudgery
of multiplication and division, of writing and of spelling;
he is vexed with problems in Euclid, he is troubled with
outline drawing, and not less with shading, but with a
devotion little short of heroism he works with all his
heart and makes wonderful progress. And these brave
young fellows who have their own living to earn, when
once they master their studies, pursue them with an application seldom equalled by those of a higher social position.
One of the Directors of the celebrated Drawing School at
Nuremberg, in Germany,—a school which has perhaps
exercised a greater influence upon industry than any other in
Europe—said to some friends and myself last spring, "Of
all the students who come here there are none who do such
good work and are such a credit to the school and themselves as the young artisans who have to depend upon their
daily labour for their bread." Go through the Science and

Art Classes at Keighley, and the masters would say the same; but the young men who come to learn the special technical knowledge connected with a certain trade, and find that they know nothing of the simple rudiments of the subject, are sorely tried; some go back manfully to the "three R's" again—but not a few give up the whole thing in despair, and leave the classes altogether.

Many youths see the importance and valuable uses of a knowledge of drawing. At the commencement of each session a fresh relay of beginners appears; they find after a few lessons that they do not make the progress they expected—for there is no royal road to excellence, all must work if they are to be successful—so they fall away, and in too many instances never try again.

It is precisely the same in elementary classes. Young men and women flock to the institute when these classes commence, scores of them can scarcely read, some can neither write nor cypher, and, after a few weeks, the difficulty of learning, shame of their ignorance, or temptations of one sort or another take a large percentage away.

In other towns a similar state of things exists, although oft-times with greater cause. I have the honour to be a member of the Executive Committee of the Yorkshire Union of Mechanics' Institutes, and on that committee I meet gentlemen from the chief centres of industry in the county, who are practically engaged in the promotion of education of this character. There are examinations conducted by the Union through the various institutes, and the most proficient members of the classes connected with those institutes compete at the examinations, so that the papers represent the work of some of the most intelligent artisans in Yorkshire. I have seen these papers, and I was told by the examiners, although some bore the marks of great natural ability, that they were humiliated beyond measure by the answers given during the last examination, which indicated an appalling want of education among the great masses of Yorkshiremen,—a want so great, that the zeal and liberality of all our voluntary institutions are quite incapable of supplying a remedy. For instance, one of the arithmetic examiners told me that, in the answers to ten questions, which did not go beyond compound division, less than 6 per 100 of the candidates received the full number of marks, and " a very large proportion failed in numeration." On being asked to write in figures, such a number as 5492, some employed nine figures for the purpose, —thus, 5000, 400, 92. In an examination in English history, in a town not far from Leeds, in which twenty-four young men and boys presented themselves, the examiner asked, " Write down any important event in the reign of Queen Elizabeth ? " and, in telling the story to me, he said, it was evident that, to the whole class, the question was a puzzler. Presently, however, one boy wrote for his answer—" *Queen Elizabeth beheaded.*" Another, whose reputation for history amongst his fellows seems to have been greater than that of the rest, wrote down an answer, which seemed to impress his neighbours as a conclusive one, for three who were nearest him copied it; the rest of the nineteen simply looked vacantly at the examiner, as if they had never heard of Queen Elizabeth before. The answer, however, which this young Macaulay had written, and which had been so faithfully copied by three others was—" *Napoleon was a great Warrio, and had to get into a big oak tree for his life.*" In the town and parish of Keighley, with a population of about 29,000, taking the calculation based on the census returns, it is estimated that there are about 2240 young men and

2450 young women, between the ages of thirteen and twenty-one. Every one of these young men and women ought, during some portion of these eight years, to go through some course of training by evening classes or otherwise, that would give purpose and directness to the education they received at school, or help them to master important practical subjects which they have imperfectly studied. Yet, what is the fact? The classes at the Mechanics' Institute have been, I believe, previous to this session, almost the only evening classes that have been open in the district. In these, there are 370 young men and 70 young women distributed over the art, science, elementary and other classes. There remain over 4000 persons of an age to profit by evening instruction, but few of whom can be educationally accounted for.

These young men and women are active somewhere, and their quick minds are receiving impressions of one kind or another. I will hopefully assume that most of the girls are undergoing some sort of useful domestic training at home in their hours of leisure; but I fear that many of the boys and young men are spending their time to no good purpose. Walk through our streets at night, see the scores of idle loiterers, hear their coarse and oft-times offensive language, look in at the drinking and singing saloons, which are rising up in this and other towns with alarming speed and popularity, and you will not need to ask further, how many of these youths spend their leisure.

I was told the other day by a practical mechanic who is well acquainted with the attainments and tastes of the men of his class, and takes a great interest in their welfare, that it might be said with safety that one third of the men employed in the machine shops of Keighley cannot read a newspaper. Although this statement appears to be discouraging, in view of the political and other responsibilities in which most of these men have, and will have, to take part, yet it is not so appalling as a remark contained in the third report of the Children's Employment Commission, which states that 86 per cent. of the girls of school age in one factory could not read.* Of course no one expects to find anything approaching such a state of things in this locality; but I am bound to say that I felt so humiliated by the discovery that the attainments of the boys and girls who go through our elementary schools were much lower than I had expected to find them, that I was most anxious to arrive at some means, beyond estimates however fair, of knowing whether the illiteracy with which they began life would continue with them during their struggles with the world. The Factory Acts have been in operation now for 25 years, and therefore we have a right to assume that most of the persons to whom I am about to allude have attended our day schools, with which we have been so well satisfied, and which I have seldom let slip an opportunity of praising. Yet in spite of what they have done, you may have some idea as to what they have left undone when I tell you that of 1,000 entries taken indiscriminately from the register of births, deaths, and marriages, in Keighley, in the year 1872, 337 names (or one in every 3) were signed with a (×) cross. We look upon those good people who marry as not the least intelligent members of the community, yet in Keighley 25 per cent. of these register their names with a cross. I would not, however, willingly record the inability of men or women to sign their names on their wedding day as

---

* Common Schools of England. Jesse Collings, p. 35

evidence against them, for it is a day when hands are often shaky and nerves unsteady. But without including these, you are aware that we have a class of respectable householders who like to admit not only daylight but gaslight into their dwellings. The Local Board of Health supplies gas to those in the town who ask for it. As you know, many of the most illiterate do not make application, so that the gas consumers include all the most intelligent people, leaving a residuum excluded; yet of those for whom the necessary forms have been filled up during the past year, 26 in every 100 have signed their names with a cross, and a great number of those who have affixed their signatures give an impression that although they have managed to write their names they would have a difficulty in writing anything else. If we exclude from these statistics the gas consumers who reside in the better houses, and include only the districts of the town inhabited by those whom we may fairly suppose have been educated in the Elementary Factory Schools, instead of having 26 per cent. we shall have nearer 50 per cent. who sign their names with a cross.

I do not wish to attach much importance to facts of this character; but at any rate they show conclusively that the system of education as practised in England up to the passing of Mr. Forster's Act of 1870, has been in every sense unsatisfactory. Under the old state of things the Government helped those districts that were best able to provide for themselves, and neglected those parishes where voluntary exertion did little. The "religious difficulty" has been the stumbling-block in the way of national education for a greater number of years than I care to reckon; the State sided with those who were willing to help themselves; the Voluntaryies opposed the State grants on principle, while unable to supply an alternative or impart enthusiasm to their own cause ; the consequence has been that the great bulk of existing national schools have been provided by Denominationalists, who are naturally opposed to, or jealous of, any movement entailing sacrifices upon them, or taking away the advantages which they at present enjoy.

But in spite of all that Denominationalists and Voluntaries have done, one is driven to the conclusion that a large proportion of English children do not attend school at all; that of those who do attend, the majority are dismissed with a most inadequate knowledge of reading, writing, and arithmetic, that no less in the large towns than in some of the agricultural districts the educational destitution has been of a most shameful character. In one district education is popular, in another it is quite the reverse, and unheeded ; in some parts of Yorkshire and Lancashire praiseworthy efforts have been made, and schools of one kind or another have not lagged far behind the requirements of the time, at least in point of accommodation. In London, however, 80,039 children, requiring elementary education and without excuse for absence, do not attend school ;* estimates made in Manchester and Birmingham are even less favourable, while in the Diocese of Norfolk there are no less than 120 parishes in which, in 1867, no day school existed.† Mr. Matthew Arnold, one of the highest educational authorities in the country, estimates that only 50 per cent. of the population of school age, are in actual attendance, while Mr. Bruce—who is always mindful to be within the mark in his assertions—fears that " at least 50 per cent. of our population are practically

---

* Report of London School Board, 1872.

† See Mr. Dent's speech on the Sixth Report of the Children's Employment Commission, 2nd April, 1867.

uneducated."* I have roughly and very imperfectly endeavoured to show the amount of scholastic training really received by the population of such towns as Keighley, although there having been no national system and no general reports from year to year to reveal our shortcomings and excellencies, I have had to trust very much to estimates on both sides.

I will now turn, however, to another part of my subject, and sketch for you the national school systems of, say Germany and Switzerland.

In a recent visit to those countries, which I made with other gentlemen of this town in order to inspect schools and inquire into the subject of education, we had special opportunities afforded of receiving information. We found that every child, from the age of six to fourteen—in some parts of Switzerland from six to sixteen — must attend school. Compulsion can be enforced by admonitions, penalties, and imprisonments; there is an elaborate machinery for exercising strict supervision over attendance, but practically the compulsory powers are never enforced, as the people themselves having experienced its advantages are its advocates, and an evasion of the law is never attempted. Education is the most popular movement in these countries. Upon whatever other questions they may disagree, there is unanimity upon this, that the first duty of the state is to be assured of the education of its children. "Education, more than anything else, has fraternised the German nation," it has counterbalanced many physical drawbacks in Switzerland, and through its influence, it is said that "the Swiss of the German Cantons are the Scotchmen of continental

---

* Questions for a Reformed Parliament, p. 144.

Europe."* "Whatever you would have appear in a nation's life, *that* you must put into its schools," was long since a motto in Germany, and the Germans seem to have thrown as much care into their development of the instruction of the people as into their military organisation, which astonished the world so much two years ago. The consequence is that kingdom rivals kingdom, town rivals town, and village rivals village in the completeness, arrangement, and efficiency of their schools. And these schools are ranged upon such a systematic plan, that the parent who intends a certain career for his child can have him educated in accordance with his intentions and within his means.

I have found it necessary, in order to make this plan thoroughly intelligible to you all, to sketch a chart, by which you can see at a glance the arrangement of the schools, and how they are graded so as to follow each other in systematic order, and in accordance with the intended career of the scholar.

The boy commences with the primary school at six, where he is taught all the elements of indispensable knowledge. He may remain, if the means and desires of his parent do not favour advancement, during eight years, the last two of which may have been worked half-time at the factory. After leaving the primary school, he will be required in Switzerland to attend the singing class† during one evening a-week till the age of sixteen. On other evenings, and during holidays and Sundays, he will have the opportunity of attending some school, such as the improvement school, trade school, building school, weaving school, agricultural school, or drawing school, which will increase his technical knowledge

---

* B. Samuelson, M.P.

† French Report on Technical Education, page 149.

of the trade upon which he has entered. All the above are schools which may be taken advantage of by the workman. Generally speaking, however, the parents of the middle classes make up their minds early as to whether their son shall receive a classical or scientific training. If the former, he is removed as soon as he can pass the entrance examination to the progymnasium and thence to the gymnasium (which corresponds to the best of our grammar schools). Here he will remain if he is intended to be a lawyer, divine, or shows the qualifications for a schoolmaster, till seventeen or eighteen, and will then complete his scholastic course by three or four years' study, till twenty-one or twenty-two, at the University. If on the other hand it is intended that he shall have a scientific training, so as to fit him for trade, or some branch of the public service, he will pass from the Primary to the Real or Practical School, where he will receive an excellent training in mathematics, physical science, drawing and modern languages, with other necessary instruction for a man of business. If after three or four years here, he wishes to continue his education to a still higher point, say as chemist, architect, or engineer, he will add a course of three or four years at the Polytechnic School, which is a scientific university, with an extensive range of studies, all of which are taught most fully and profoundly.

In Switzerland, the girl will have an opportunity, after leaving the primary school, of attending the drawing school, or of taking up certain special sciences. In every country district there must also be a school for needlework and other female occupations.* If the means of her parent will allow,

---

* French Report on Technical Instruction, page 150.

the pupil will proceed from the primary to the higher secondary school, and, if training for a learned profession, will complete her studies at the University.

The primary schools of Germany are, as a rule, built by the municipality of each town out of the rates and taxes, and the deficiency above the cost of fees is made up in the same manner. The municipality also generally defrays the cost of the Real or Practical Schools. The State supplies the Polytechnic Schools and Universities, renders considerable assistance to the *Gymnasien*, and jointly with the municipality to many of the industrial schools. Of these there is a variety in different parts of Germany, which have been established for the sole purpose of improving existing trades and of introducing new trades into poor and populous districts, unable to find a profitable field for their labour. Thus there are schools of this kind for lace-making and hosiery, the manufacture of carpets, clock and watchmaking, painting on enamel, porcelain and earthenware, straw-plaiting and fancy weaving. Some of these have greatly developed the resources of the country, and given rise to considerable trades.* In fact, so clearly is the principle recognised that education develops industry, that although the strictest economy is exercised in general expenditure, no outlay seems to be too great for the furtherance of any educational project that will make land or labour more productive in any promising locality.

And just as school buildings are supplied by rates and taxes, so also the Germans and Swiss " pay taxes in lieu of school fees, which sink to a trifling sum. Those parents who prefer a private school pay towards the support of the public schools at the same time that they meet their separate school

---

* French Report, p. 10.

bills. In any comparison of the cost of education in England and Germany, this difference must be borne in mind. Here, each parent, at least in the middle classes, pays for himself. In Germany, the parent pays little for the schooling of his own children, but he is subject throughout life, and the childless citizen is equally subject to education rates and education taxes."* To the parent who has several children, a number of whom may be attending school at the same time, the advantage of this system is apparent; he has no large school bills to meet; in fact, the principle is closely analogous to that of our building societies, where a heavy expenditure is met by gradual and continuous payments. "When it is stated that the cost of the primary schools is defrayed by the municipality, the difference between the sources of the municipal fund in England and Germany must be borne in mind. The communal income in Prussia is derived mainly from an income tax levied on all receipts and earnings whatsoever. The day labourer pays on his wages of ten shillings a-week, the maid-servant on her wages of £5 a-year. Consequently every one pays a fair share towards the expenses of public education. A corresponding vote out of the municipal rates of an English town would be a tax on the middle classes exclusively."*

"Education on the continent is gratuitous to the very poor, and of nominal cost to artisans. The fees for primary schools in Prussia are assessed by the local authorities and vary with the means of the parent. The maximum is fifteen thalers (£2 4s.) per annum; the minimum, one groschen, (1½d.) per week, or 6s. 6d. per annum for each child between six and fourteen. In Berlin the average cost to the muni-

---

* Unofficial Comments on Education, p. 11.

cipality of each child in the elementary schools is £1 per annum, and the school expenses (exclusive of fees and grants) constitute 12 per cent of the whole municipal charges." *

At the age of six the little boys and girls begin their first experience of attending a public elementary school. Most of them have learnt their letters at the infant school or at home before this time, for home training in Germany is not neglected.

The elementary schools of the towns which we visited greatly impressed us by their stateliness, stability of construction and internal arrangements. All the buildings are furnished with every requisite for their great purpose, divided into class rooms in accordance with the number of scholars,— not more than fifty pupils being taught in one room,—while in addition to these there are museum, gymnasium, masters' rooms, and a large and handsome hall, where school festivals and annual examinations are held.

The teachers are all men of high attainments, and are required to go through a special training in order to gain a certificate of capacity to teach. As a rule, one master does not teach more than two or three subjects, and upon these he has generally so concentrated his energies as to understand them thoroughly; in fact, it is stated that "no experience or length of service enables a teacher to conduct any class not specified in his certificate," and no amount of knowledge will render any man acceptable who cannot satisfactorily impart that knowledge to others.

In the grounds of an elementary school at Zurich we saw trees flourishing, trimly kept flower beds, and a pretty fountain. As a rule, however, playgrounds are not large,

---

* Unofficial Comments on Education, p. 12.

nor are they used so heartily for games by the boys as our English playgrounds are. In England, time, energies, and thought are sacrificed by many boys to cricket, while the studious ones remain at their books during the play hour inside. This is not so in Germany; at the ordinary schools there is no cricket—and in their sports generally they seem to lack that energy and manliness so characteristic of English schoolboys—but all must turn out at stated times and have gymnastic lessons under a master who is often a military man, so that the directors have a guarantee that no boy escapes regular exercise and physical development.

The manufacturing town of Chemnitz, in Saxony, is very like Keighley in its combination of trades—wool and iron—and many of the yarns spun in Keighley are there woven into manufactured goods, and then sent to compete with those woven here. The town is rapidly extending, and we learned that as new streets are being mapped out, the authorities make choice of the most favourable sites for schools, which thus keep pace with the population. Among the educational curiosities which we saw at Chemnitz was an elementary school, containing fifty-four class-rooms, and attended by over four thousand children. Among these are the younger children and half-timers, yet the arrangement is such that all the scholars attending at one time can sit at their desks and, if necessary, receive a writing lesson with the light coming in at the left hand of each pupil. No one would have believed, in traversing the spacious corridors of this vast establishment, that the school was in operation. There were no mischievous stragglers, not the least uproar, yet every one of these numerous rooms was occupied by happy looking boys and girls, diligently prosecuting their studies. Nothing could be more interesting than to see the classes of the youngest children, who were invariably taught by men possessing a large experience, together with a wonderful power of making the simplest lessons attractive. By the aid of pictures, natural objects, little stories, and a variety of methods, all tending to the development of their thinking faculties, the lessons were made so pleasant as to command their complete attention and enthusiasm. Throughout all the classes there seemed to be the same mastery of the subject by the teacher, and the same enthusiasm and application on the part of the scholar. All subjects that come within the recognised school course receive careful attention, and I think I shall never forget the singing of a chorale of Mendelssohn's, in four parts, by boys and girls of about twelve years of age, in an elementary school. It was evident that not only in time, but in tune and modulation, the children were receiving a thorough musical training.

Mr. Bernhard Samuelson, M.P., who visited many continental schools in 1867, says, in his report, that the hours he spent in attending the classes of certain schools would long remain in his memory as the most delightful incidents of his journey. Our experience was exactly the same. He says,—"The lessons consisted of animated exercises and conversations, in which the teachers and pupils joined with equal zest. The attention of the youngest and least intelligent scholar never flagged for an instant. Nowhere else is the art of forming and developing the minds of young children understood and practised in such perfection as in Germany. Nowhere else has it received a name. In nearly every state and canton the teachers of the elementary and higher schools are trained in the same establishment, and have received the same instruction,

if not in degree at least in kind; and¦ an effort is everywhere made to secure the most competent men for the
Volksschulen of the smaller communes possessing no upper
school, so that the children in them may enjoy some share
of the higher instruction which the secondary schools
would have afforded them in more favoured localities."

Shakspeare, in his Seven Ages, has vividly depicted the
English schoolboy of his day and of ours :—

> The whining schoolboy, with his satchel,
> And shining morning face, creeping like snail
> Unwillingly to school.

But the modern German and Swiss schoolboys seem to be of
a different type, and attend school rather as a pleasure than
a duty; in fact, to see the boys and girls, some in broadcloth,
others in clogs and leathern "jumps," or aprons such as
cobblers wear, but all with knapsacks' strapped to their
shoulders, trudging cheerfully to school at seven o'clock in the
morning, both in fair weather and in foul, is not one of the
least suggestive of the many sights to be witnessed in the
towns of Germany and Switzerland.

The generality of children belonging to the labouring
population receive the whole of their education in the
elementary school. In the small schools the classes are mixed;
in the large ones the boys and girls are generally separated
at the age of ten or eleven. All are expected to advance to
the highest class during their eight years' course. Backward
pupils often get up their lessons out of school hours with a
master. In the manufacturing towns, some of the children
commence working half-time at the age of twelve—although
very few are thus employed—and continue until fourteen; but
many are required to attend the evening classes and Sunday
schools till sixteen, so that they may pursue with greater

directness the study of drawing and the sciences; and in the Canton Zurich of Switzerland, all must attend the singing-classes during one evening in the week. In some of the large towns there are three classes of elementary schools—upper, middle and lower,—in the upper of which the teaching and fees are higher, while the lowest is usually attended by the poorest of the children and the half-timers; but these three classes of elementary schools are not common, and I believe do not exist in Switzerland.

All elementary schools teach the ground-work and basis of knowledge, and the curriculum consists of reading, writing, arithmetic, religion, geography, history, drawing and the elements of the sciences.

In religion, there are, broadly speaking, but two sects recognised by the State in Germany — Evangelical and Catholic — and the instruction is usually imparted by specially appointed teachers. The majority of the pupils have a separate lesson in the large room of the school, while the minority, at stated times out of the regular school hours, march in procession to service at the nearest church of the requisite creed. As for the ordinary school lessons, "complaint is made by parents that religion is the one thing which a German schoolmaster teaches by rote."*

One strong point in both the German and Swiss plans of elementary education, which I have so roughly sketched, is this. Where schools are needed, there schools are planted; and in towns, schools which we should call very large are almost universal, while in country districts the necessarily small schools are placed so as to be as convenient as possible for the surrounding inhabitants. Probably in a town of the

---

* Unofficial Comments on Education, p. 15.

population of Keighley there would not be more than one or two primary schools instead of four or five, and these being large, a museum, gymnasium, and other requisites could be more economically and better supplied than in smaller schools. The question is very much one of class-rooms and teachers. Whereas in English schools, where the scholars are mostly taught in one large room, it is seldom that the buildings are erected of more than one storey ; in Switzerland, on the contrary, the schools are often three or four storeys high, and this method is not only more convenient but more economical. Under this arrangement a director can organise and control a large school—say of 800 or 1,000 pupils—almost as easily as a small one, the scholars can be classified in accordance with their ages and abilities, the classes are more even and therefore more easily taught;—they advance more rapidly ; and the teachers can devote their attention to those subjects for which they possess the highest qualification. Further, the pupils, changing every hour from room to room and from teacher to teacher, find their faculties brightened and their limbs exercised in the fresh air of the open corridor, and reap the benefit of a thorough ventilation of the class-rooms. In the Saxon town of Meerane, which Keighley yarns and machinery are wonderfully developing, a new elementary school was being built at the time of our visit, and, rather than that the children should be neglected, thirty cottages were being utilised for their instruction. We were here very hospitably entertained by an English gentleman, who had gone from this neighbourhood to Germany as an artisan many years before, and had been prosperous. Like other English residents, he was enthusiastic in his praises of the schools and of the intelligence, sobriety, and honesty of the people. He amused us greatly by a statement which we ought not to have wondered at. He said that on his last visit to this district, he had occasion one Saturday night to walk through the streets of Ivegate and Westgate, in Bradford, and that he was so shocked with the amount of drunkenness and vice which he saw at every step, and with the filthy and obscene language which he was compelled to hear, that he left Bradford as quickly as he could, for he feared that the whole town was going as fast as possible to the Devil. He had certainly not been accustomed to such sights and sounds in Saxony. Unfortunately, however, they are not uncommon in the streets of Keighley; and yet, in our self-righteousness, we close our eyes and pass by on the other side, without ever being the victims of such strange fears as those of our friend, who, after a few years' absence, had returned to see the progress of our civilisation.

> So much a long communion tends
> To make us what we are.

I will now hastily advance to the next links in the State Education of Germany, and say a few words of the secondary schools, open to boys from ten to eighteen, who can only be admitted by passing an entrance examination. Of these schools I have shown to you that there are two kinds, for, after the primary schools, education begins to branch off into the special kinds required by professional, scientific, and commercial men; nor are there any towns without these schools, or some modification of them. The pupils are mostly the sons of well-to-do tradesmen, manufacturers, professional men and landed proprietors. Some, however, are poor boys, who in virtue of having obtained scholarships are receiving their higher education for nothing. In fact, it is no figure of speech to say that in these Gymnasien and Real Schools the prince and the peasant sit side by side on tho same form.* The fees range from £5 to £10 a year, and, unlike the middle-class schools of England, there are no extras.

These secondary schools enjoy great and well-deserved popularity, not only because of the superior training they give, but because of the fact that they can grant certificates admitting students to the universities and polytechnic schools for a still more advanced course of study; and also certificates entitling pupils to present themselves for rank of officers in the army, and reduce from three years to one the term of military service. We thus see how it is that even the poor are willing to make great sacrifices in order to send their children to higher schools where they may obtain an education which confers such valuable prizes. Private schools have no chance against such institutions as these, and they are naturally very few in Germany. "The want of suitable furniture and apparatus, of searching inspection, and, above all, of a sufficiently numerous staff of highly-qualified teachers" renders it impossible that they should enjoy much popular favour. "In Switzerland, the private schools subsist mainly on English patronage, and here they appear to sink to their lowest level."†

Respecting German Universities, it is not necessary that I should make any comment, but the Polytechnic Schools, which afford the higher professional, commercial and scientific instruction, are splendid institutions, in which no desirable requisite for the thorough and profound cultivation of any

---

* The director of the Real School at Dresden told us that a young prince from Russia sat next to a scholarship boy whose parents were just removed from pauperism.

† See Mr. Matthew Arnold's "Report on Secondary Education in foreign countries," 1868, p. 619.

branch of scientific study is wanting. They are built, furnished and almost entirely maintained by the state, and in no department of education has the rivalry of different states manifested itself so lavishly as in the foundation of these buildings and in providing them with highly-trained professors. Students— many of whom are free—are admitted on passing the necessary examination, and arranged according to their intended pursuits, a choice of subjects is made from an extensive range, or a certain fixed course may be accepted. It would be quite impossible, within the limits of a sketch such as this, to give any idea of the majestic size, or the arrangements, say, of the Zurich Polytechnic. Among the professors are numbered several men of European reputation. The collections in the several museums are remarkably extensive, and are made to look still more imposing by their excellent arrangement. The zoological, geological, mineralogical, and antiquarian collections are valuable and instructive. In the department of architecture, there are models and drawings of the best buildings of the world, and the collection of sculpture, with its carefully assorted and superb casts of the great works of Greece and Rome, gives in itself a history of sculpture from the earliest to the present time. In the mechanical department there are drawings and models of engines of every conceivable kind. There are hundreds of small machines, most of them made by the masters and students, which exhibit almost every complicated mechanical contrivance, and can be worked by hand. The models of agricultural implements are not less remarkable than the actual examples of agricultural produce, while there is an extensive botanical garden connected with the establishment, and a large astronomical observatory fixed on a neighbouring hill. The chemical laboratory is a large erection separate from the main building. Though complete and efficient, it is surpassed by others which we saw, and particularly by Hoffman's famous laboratory at Berlin, which in itself is larger than the Keighley Mechanics' Institute and Schools of Science and Art put together. You cannot but be astounded to hear that German and Swiss Governments provide such splendid institutions for the higher education of their peoples; but you will marvel to hear that for regular pupils the fees charged for all these advantages do not exceed, at the Zurich Polytechnic, £4 a year—excepting a small sum for laboratory and workshop practice—and that no extras are required from foreigners.*

Imperfectly and very roughly, I have endeavoured to describe the national schools of Germany and Switzerland. Some will say, Figures are all very well, but do the children really attend school, and what are the results of all this education? Let us take the question of attendance first. We asked everywhere, "Are there any children of school age who are not at school?" The answer invariably was "No!" In one of the largest elementary schools which we visited, and which was chiefly attended by the children of poor parents and half-timers, we asked particularly if parents resorted to tricks, as they do in Keighley, in order that their children might escape attendance. The Director was astonished at the question; he stated that he had never the slightest difficulty either with parents or employers, and that such tricks were never attempted. He showed us his register to prove how regular in attendance all his scholars were, and we came upon one case, by no means an exceptional one, of a poor boy who had attended school for eight years,

* French Commission on Technical Instruction, p. 158.

and had only absented himself for four days—and these were days of sickness—during the whole time. In the large machinery and manufacturing establishments which we visited, employers said that there was a difficulty in persuading parents to allow their children to work before the age of fourteen, and as a rule they preferred not to employ them before that age, as they considered that any gain in manual skill and dexterity acquired in the two years of half-time was more than compensated by the increased intelligence gained during the extra schooling. At the gigantic establishment of Mr. Krupp, at Essen, in Westphalia,—the largest in the world—where upwards of ten thousand men are employed in the different processes of steel casting and the manufacture of artillery, we were told that not a single half-timer is employed, and no boys are admitted until after the age of fourteen.

In the state of Baden, "a French sportsman bent upon amusement, in vain offered a florin a-piece for boys to attend him as beaters. The parents replied that they had to go to school."* In the same State, the law enforcing the attendance of apprentices at evening and Sunday schools is so strict, that the Burgomaster, or if needful, the clergyman of the township can "pronounce penalties against masters who neglect the duty of sending their apprentices to the schools."†

As to the results of this education, in Würtemberg it is said, " There is not a peasant or kitchen maid who cannot read,

---

* "Questions for a Reformed Parliament," p. 150.

† The Sunday Schools are different in character from ours, and do not, I am sorry to say, as a rule supply religious instruction; they offer to artizans an opportunity of studying science and drawing at the expense of the municipality. French Commission on Technical Instruction, p. 182.

write and cypher well." " Recruits are put through an examination, and the parents are responsible if their son cannot write." In Saxony it is said " There is not a child to be found who has had no schooling." Nassau "boasts that it has not one illiterate person in the duchy."

The French report of 1863 gives a curious instance of Prussian vigilance. " An officer, whose duty it was to give military instruction to the Landwehr at Potsdam, discovered, in the course of twelve years, three recruits who could neither read nor write. Their case was thought so extraordinary that an investigation was ordered, when it appeared that they were three sons of boatmen who had been born on the river, and had passed their early lives in voyaging up and down the stream, never stopping at any one place."

In another report, I find that " the colonel of a regiment in one of the minor states of Germany,* having ascertained that, out of a contingent of 800 men recently sent to him, four individuals could not read, the fact appeared so extraordinary that an inquiry was held in order to ascertain the cause." In comparing these illustrations with the state of things existing in this country, I beg of you to bear in mind the statement which I made, that, broadly speaking, nearly 30 per 100 in the town of Keighley cannot write; but an extract which I cut from a Liverpool paper some weeks ago reveals worse cases than any I have yet recorded. A "Vicar" writes: "This morning I performed two marriages at the church of my little parish, and, when the parties came to sign the registers, I found that of the whole eight—that is to say, the four persons married and their witnesses—not one

---

* French Commission on Technical Instruction, &c., p. 3.

could write." We frequently read announcements of a character approaching to this and smile; in Germany they would rouse the nation.

The benefits of the training in modern languages received by the Germans is exemplified to us every day by the fact that nearly the whole of the Continental export trade in cotton, worsted yarns and manufactured goods in Manchester and Bradford, amounting in annual value to several millions sterling, is in the hands of Germans, who are represented in the manufacturing centres abroad by their own agents. The trade in English goods is not usually conducted on such a plan; all the world over it is mostly in the hands of Englishmen, and it is often alleged as a reason why it is not so in this instance, that Germans are taught English and other modern languages at school, while the English, as a rule, are not taught any language but their own.

With regard to the moral and social aspects of the question, I find that " in Switzerland a reformed system of education has almost emptied the gaols." " In the Grand Duchy of Baden, where efforts were made in 1834 for the improvement of education, the number of prisoners fell in eight years (1854 to 1861) from 1426 to 691; the number of thefts from 1009 became 460; pauperism decreased by one-fourth, and gaols had to be closed."

In Bavaria, an improved education was followed by a remarkable decrease of criminal offences. " In Germany generally the number of criminal convictions was diminished between 1827 and 1862 by 30 per cent." So it has been proved, almost universally, that in proportion as money has been wisely spent on education, in the same proportion have pauperism and criminal offences declined; as the education taxes have increased, so in a greater proportion have the general taxes in the aggregate decreased. In the smaller German States, while the total taxation per head is much lower than that of other countries, the proportion for education is much higher. While in Saxony the cost of public instruction is 140 per cent. higher than that of France, the total contribution of each individual to the taxes is nearly 160 per cent. higher in France than in Saxony*—a most startling difference; and probably a similar comparison between Saxony and this country would not be less startling against us. Truly, the words of the French Minister, in advocating a liberal allowance for education, expressed more than a mere eloquent sentiment when he said, "We shall save in prisons what we spend in schools."

I doubt not that many of you are ready to say—"Yes; all this is very well, but how is it that, in spite of this superior training and culture, England still holds her own among the nations in commerce; and how is it, that in her manufactured goods, she can compete successfully against them all in the markets of the world?"

I, for one, am not prepared, as a citizen of our great country, to yield one inch of the legitimate position which England holds as a manufacturing community. The work done in this district is probably as good as any of the kind in Germany; but I do not think that it is much better. Now, it is not many years since the Germans were immeasurably behind us in the production of almost every important article of manufacture; it is not so to the same extent now, and there is no doubt that education on the continent generally is fast making up for many material advantages possessed by this country.

---

* See French Commission on Technical Instruction, p. 29.

Great natural resources are in our favour, and these have been supplemented by many blessings not enjoyed by other countries. Whilst for generations past, the continent of Europe was being impoverished by desolating wars and revolutions, which constantly removed the flower of the nations from peaceful labour, this country of ours—described by Shakspeare 250 years ago, as " this precious stone set in the silver sea,"—secure in its insular position, enjoying domestic peace and freedom, possessing in great quantities coal and iron—the sinews of wealth, favoured by situation and climate, and above all, peopled by a hardy, energetic race of men, was not slow in taking advantage of her resources and opportunities. England, by the sheer force of circumstances, became " a nation of shopkeepers ;" she manufactured for the world, and she did her work so much better, and so much cheaper than it could be done elsewhere, that for a time the world seemed satisfied to allow her a monopoly. She was wondrously assisted too by the genius of a few men who revolutionised the industries of the country by their discoveries and inventions, and gave us a glorious prestige. We should never forget that Watt, Stephenson, Arkwright, and a host of industrial pioneers to whom the world will be for ever indebted, were Englishmen.

Under free trade our products were distributed over the globe, our ships brought back raw material, and capital poured into the country. In the meantime the nations of the continent took advantage of intervals of peace to develop their industries. Free trade has given to them our machinery and the advantages of our great inventions. Like us they have coal and iron, and they have hard working men, nearly all of whom, a generation since, had received a good general education.

E

It is unnecessary for me to trace step by step the rapid advancement in commerce which some nations have made during the past twenty years. The exhibition of 1851 revealed to the world our wonderful supremacy, a supremacy which astonished ourselves. True we were behind in some departments of manufacture in which taste and design were important features, and a few zealous patriots who saw the cause,—headed by the late Prince Consort— determined that if possible this state of things should be remedied. They saw that the workman must know something of the principles of art, that he must be taught drawing; and to their efforts we owe the formation of the Museum at South Kensington, and the establishment of the Schools of Art which are now scattered throughout the country. But in the great iron industries, as in other manufactures upon which commendation had been so freely lavished, where immense capital had been accumulated and machinery was superseding the labour of man, we were content to go on as we were, self-conscious of our unrivalled superiority. After the exhibition of 1851 foreigners, and especially Germans, went to their homes with a conviction that it was useless to attempt to compete with us in mineral productions, and that they must begin by training the faculties of their men. In addition to the good primary education which they had already received, they began systematically to carry out on a vast national scale, what had already been attempted in a limited degree, a scheme of technical education, spreading everywhere through the land the class of schools and colleges that was most needed to help the industries of the localities. And with what results? The exhibition of 1862 revealed a state of things which was not expected. Our neighbours, one after another, had advanced with wonderful rapidity; we were actually beginning to be rivalled in the manufacture of machinery and other articles which we had long considered as specialities of our own. There were not wanting those who gave forth the note of warning; but manufacturers who saw these things for themselves pointed to the demand which still kept up for their goods, and laughed at the so-called alarmists. Orders still came in abundantly, they were realizing large profits, and, with great capital at their command and a well earned connection to fall back upon, many of them continued in the old way, and might be compared to the razor seller who didn't care whether or not his razors would shave so long as they would sell.

It was the International Exhibition of Paris, in 1867, that brought the people of England face to face with the fact that as a manufacturing nation, we were overtaken in almost every branch of industry by one or more of the continental states; and that even our name and fame, which had blinded our customers in reference to the proficiency of others, were ceasing to prop up our tottering supremacy any longer.

We all know that we have to depend for almost everything upon our trade, and so serious was this matter considered that eminent jurors were appointed by our Government to make a thorough investigation at the Paris Exhibition and elsewhere of the products and manufactures of different nations, so as to trace their rapid improvement to its source. The Society of Arts sent out workmen representing various trades with the same object. Some gentlemen sifted out the matter at the fountain-head, visiting continental factories and workshops. Mr. Bernhard Samuelson, M.P., began an inquiry at home, and, direct from the factories and workshops of England, he proceeded to Paris, examined the productions of the different nations there exhibited, after which he visited the principal workshops and establishments in France, Germany, and Switzerland, where many of the best works which he had seen at the Exhibition were produced.

The reports of the jurors and of the workmen appointed by the Society of Arts were published, and will be familiar to many of you, while Mr. Samuelson's letter to the Committee of Council on Education was printed by order of the House of Commons. It is not necessary for me to quote from these voluminous documents—although I would advise all who have not read them to do so—which are startlingly unanimous upon one point, that the great progress made by those states whose competition was most to be feared was due, in a great measure, to the fact that the workmen received a sound elementary education, supplemented by a training in the arts and sciences bearing upon their trades. There was unanimity also in the warning that unless we in England adopted a system which should give similar results, we should most certainly lose our commercial superiority. The question was taken up by Parliament, and a Committee was appointed in 1868 to inquire into the state of scientific instruction in England, and our manufacturing position as compared with that of other countries. A ponderous blue book, containing most valuable evidence, confirmed, in the main, the views of the jurors.*

An interesting illustration of the general principles advocated in these reports is furnished by the Art Schools, which, since 1851, have been established in all parts of England. At the exhibition of 1862, one of the most encouraging

---

* Report on Scientific Instruction, July 15, 1868.

features for us was the decided improvement which had been made since 1851 in art workmanship.[*] In the production of such articles as pottery, jewellery, ornamental brass and iron work, furniture, carpets, lace, &c., the improvement that had taken place was so marked, that the manufacturers of the objects in question were applied to for their opinion, as to the influence which the newly-organised schools of art and classes had exercised upon this progress. The inquiry revealed conclusively, that the faculty of design is as prominent in the Englishman as in others, when it has a chance of development; and it is very remarkable that, although art-training had scarcely taken root in the country, its influence was considered to be proportionately as great upon English industry as that of the foreigner in his more systematic training had been upon the industries of the continent.

The fact of this country being separated from the rest of Europe by some miles of deep sea, as well as by our unfamiliarity with continental languages, renders us partly oblivious of what takes place in their inner social and commercial life. The great bulk of the people of England do not believe that the Swiss and German systems of education are more efficient than our own, neither will they believe that this country is in any danger from foreign competition in trade. But let us not deceive ourselves; the old proverb: "It is too late to lock the stable door when the horse is stolen," furnishes a little food for thought in national as well as domestic affairs. Had the French thought a little less of past glory, before the late war, and taken a little more pains to measure the strength of their opponents, or their own weakness, they

---

[*] Report on the Employment of Students of Schools of Art, &c., 1863.

might have been saved the terrific loss and the deep humiliation which they now suffer and which we all deplore.

There is such concurrent testimony of eminent men who are alarmed by the strides which others are making in consequence of their higher intelligence, that I scarcely know whose opinion you will consider most influential. Perhaps that of Mr. Mundella, M.P., from circumstances which he explains, will be accounted as important as any that I can quote. Mr. Mundella says, "The branch of industry with which I have been connected for thirty years, is the manufacturing of hosiery. I am the managing partner, employing 5000 workpeople; with establishments in Nottingham, Derby, and Loughborough, employing 4000, and with branches at Chemnitz and Pausa, in Saxony, employing about 700 persons. I have for four or five years past been increasingly alarmed for our industrial supremacy, and my experience of the Paris Exhibition has only confirmed and strengthened my fears. . . . . I am of opinion that Englishmen possess more energy, enterprise, and inventiveness, than any other European nation. The best machines in my trade now at work in France and Germany are the inventions of Englishmen, but are there constructed and improved by men who have had the advantage of a superior industrial education. At the largest establishments in Paris these machines are constructed and improved on thorough scientific principles, under the superintendence of a young man, who, I was informed, took high honours at the school of the Government in Paris. . . . Precisely the same thing is taking place in Saxony; but the Saxons are, in respect of education, both primary and industrial, much in advance of the French, and in my branch, they are our most formidable rivals. . . . The contrast betwixt the workpeople of Saxony and England, engaged in the same trade, is most humiliating. I have had statistics taken of various workshops and rooms in factories in this district, and the frightful ignorance they reveal is disheartening and appalling. . . . . In Saxony our manager, an Englishman of superior intelligence, and greatly interested in education, during a residence of seven years, has never met with a workman who cannot read and write— not in the limited and imperfect manner in which the majority of the English artisans are said to read and write, but with a freedom and familiarity that enables them to enjoy reading, and to conduct their correspondence in a creditable and often superior style. Some of the sons of our poorest workmen in Saxony are receiving a technical education at the Polytechnic Schools, such as the sons of our manufacturers cannot hope to obtain. . . . . I am of opinion that the English workman is gradually losing the race, through the superior intelligence which foreign governments are carefully developing in their artizans. . . . . The education of Germany is the result of a national organisation, which compels every peasant to send his children to school, and afterwards affords the opportunity of acquiring such technical knowledge as may be useful in the department of industry to which they are destined." The concluding sentences ought to carry great weight:—"If we are to maintain our position in industrial competition, we must oppose to this national organisation one equally effective and complete; if we continue the fight with our present voluntary system, we shall be defeated; generations hence we shall be struggling with ignorance, squalor, pauperism and crime; but, with a system of national education, made compulsory, and supplemented with art and industrial education, I believe, within twenty years, England would possess the most intelligent and inventive artisans in the world."*

The importance of such evidence cannot be over-estimated by thinking men. I can personally vouch for the great and patriotic interest taken in education by the representative of Mr. Mundella's firm in Saxony, to whom my companions and I are indebted for much kindness and information. Mr. Mundella recently said: " Germany is a giant in his cradle ; what will he be in a quarter of a century hence, and where will our countrymen stand in comparison with him, if we do not make up for lost time, and keep up with him in the race ?"

Recent events confirm these opinions, and I well remember in the spring of 1871, while travelling in Germany, when the victorious hosts were returning from the wars, often hearing in effect this statement :—" France has kept us in fear for years; we dared not to extend our commerce or invest our capital to the full, because we knew not how soon the enemy would be upon us, but now that we have driven him from our door and barricaded him within his own borders, we can develope our industries without fear; we have astonished the nations by our proficiency in the arts of war—we will let them see what we can do in the arts of peace."

And, true to this boast, the industries of Germany are extending on every hand. In a recent visit my companion and I found several districts enjoying unexampled prosperity. The gigantic steel works of Mr. Krupp, at Essen, in Westphalia, were increasing in a most extraordinary

---

* Quoted by J. Scott Russell, Technical Education, p. 96-98.

manner. The builders could not keep pace with the demand for houses; temporary erections were utilised by hundreds of artisans, who (we were told) were living on the Rochdale co-operative principle; and although over 10,000 men were employed, our conductor informed us that work would readily be given to 1000 more if they would make application.

In the manufacturing districts of Saxony new factories were being erected, and the towns were increasing in population. Additions were being made to the works of Messrs. Kramer Klatt & Co., of Nuremberg, who employ 4000 men; and at the works of Messrs. Hartmann & Co., Chemnitz, another extensive establishment, where we saw nearly 4000 men at work, a new shed, 600 feet long, was being built. We were told at two of these places—the matter was not alluded to at the third—that it would require years to complete the orders then upon their books. These establishments are all of comparatively recent growth, and it is only lately that their work has begun to tell upon that of this country. To witness the extensive employment of machinery in all departments of labour, the arrangement of the workshops, the manifest determination to do everything well, is conclusive evidence that their influence must increase; and in proof of this I need only allude to such a firm as Messrs. Hartmann & Co. The machine work is very similar in class to that of our own district; yet the mechanics are employed for longer hours than the mechanics of Keighley, and their wages are lower. But this is not all. The principal of the firm, who may be called the Platt of Germany, lays it down as a rule that no apprentice shall enter the establishment who does not at the same time go through the science classes of the magnificent Trade School of the town.

Everywhere is education recognised as the handmaid of industry. And while upon this subject, allow me to give you the testimony of our English Platt, the late M.P. for Oldham, and one of the largest employers of labour in the country, whom I remember to have made a statement two or three years ago to this effect—that with all our advantages of situation, climate, and resources, we were likely to be out-stripped in the race of commerce by other nations; our only hope was in the better education of our people.

From the French Report of Technical Education in Germany, I gather that the importance of a knowledge of drawing is proved by the fact, that in the little kingdom of Würtemberg, the establishment of 400 drawing schools during the preceding ten years, had "already led to very decided improvements in the manufactures of the country." The influence of the drawing school at Nuremberg, and of those with which it is connected, have diffused such a knowledge of art throughout the whole district, as to give a wonderful impulse to the manufacture of children's toys,—"with which Nuremberg supplies the whole world"—and which are "made in the cottages of the mountainous districts of the country. They find employment for the whole population, from children of tender age as soon as they can handle a knife, to their parents; and this home manufacture, which does not interfere with field work, contributes greatly to the prosperity of a country naturally poor and sterile." The "Parisian manu-facturers of toys and fancy articles are still in this respect, undeniably, inferior to their Nuremberg rivals" (p. 11). We are also told that a workshop for cotton spinning temporarily installed in the Conservatory of Arts and Trades, in Paris, in 1810, "helped to train a considerable number of workmen, who afterwards spread that now important industry through-out the country." The Industrial Schools of Silesia and the Grand Duchy of Baden introduced new trades into poor and populous districts, revived trades that were in a declining state, and improved others. Results no less favourable have "been obtained in Belgium, and in the province of West Flanders, where the nuisance of mendicity has been totally abated by the organisation of sixty communal weaving schools."

The German Weaving Schools deserve a lengthened description, but I will bo brief. The one at Chemnitz is a handsome building erected jointly by the state and municipality. It contains from twenty to thirty hand-looms for different kinds of patterns, a small steam engine, and eleven power looms, of which one bore the familiar name of Geo. Hattersley & Sons, Keighley, and another the name of Geo. Hodgson, Bradford. The art of designing, the composition of colours, and all the processes of transferring designs to the loom, &c., are taught minutely, and in one of the factories we visited, where figured damasks were being woven in colours, we found, on inquiry, that the overlookers and principal weavers had attended the school. One large manufacturer, who, as a youth, had gone through the school, showed us his book of designs and calculations, and also frankly confessed, that through the influence of this and other training, he had been able, in a tour through England, to sketch from memory, in a book which he showed to us, the plans and arrangements of shafting, looms and other details of many factories which he had seen, and with some of which we ourselves were familiar. The same manufacturer showed us beautiful goods from yarns spun in Keighley, which successfully compete in England with those woven in this district; and as an evidence that they were in demand, he was on that day about to have a grand festival in honour of the completion of another new mill.

At the Stuttgart Weaving School, when the students—who have previously worked at their trade—" have thoroughly acquired the theory of weaving in all its details and applications, the most proficient of them, who are bound to study French and English, are sent to France and England, with a grant of money to work in the best factories, and for the sake of improvement. On returning to their own country they become competent overseers in workshops and factories."*

We must remember that all these efforts on the part of Continental States are made with the object of giving moral and mental strength and culture to the people, and of attaining a sound commercial and manufacturing position. That they have been to a great exent successful I think we must all admit. If such means are so powerful in attaining an industrial position, they will not be less powerful in maintaining one, and we must use them if we are determined still to take the lead.

Up to this time there has been a wonderful difference in the labour market, arising from the character and feeling of the labourers themselves. I yield to no man in admiration of many of the qualities of the English artisan. He possesses a natural inventiveness, a fidelity to work, a power of " getting along," and of making a " spurt " on occasion, which I have failed to see in his Continental rivals. His wits also have been sharpened by the constant demand for labour; he has thus felt himself to be a valuable member of the community. He has known, too, that if he left one situation there were two more ready for him; and the feeling has made him manly and independent, but in too many

---

* French Report on Technical Instruction, p. 170.

instances careless and profligate also. In thousands of cases the money that has come so easily has been spent recklessly; drink, the national curse, ruins many of our most able-bodied men, and families are constantly pauperised and degraded because of the ignorance and sin of parents.

So far as I am able to judge, this is not the case in Germany or Switzerland. The countries are poor, natural resources are few, labourers till lately have been plentiful, and I believe that they have not quite got rid of the hereditary fear that there will not be plenty of work to follow that which they have in hand. They have been accustomed, in past times, to be put on the stint, in accordance with the whim or necessity of employers. They seem, therefore—to use a phrase common in this district—to "nurse" their work, and not get it through their hands as Englishmen do, although I do not think that this charge equally applies to the great industrial workshops and factories which I have specially mentioned. They know also that we possess very great advantages over them—our insular position, wealth, resources, and freedom. They know that the Englishman may work through life at his trade, without ever dreaming of being disturbed by a foreign foe, or of being called upon to defend his shores, while they have to give three years of their prime —from twenty to twenty-three, just when aspirations for the future are strongest—to severe military training, and that they may be liable to be called upon at any day to leave their families and their homes, and take up arms in defence of their country, or for the invasion of another. Industrially, this must be a disadvantage which it is impossible for us to calculate. They have felt that competition with us under such circumstances has been hopeless, and a moral feeling of this kind is always depressing; but supposing that they all discovered, what some have found out already, that we are so far weighted by ignorance, pauperism, and other drags upon our industry, as to make it worth their while to enter the lists against us, every man making an effort? To do this a little enthusiasm is only needed. Mr. Mundella's "giant" has only to rouse himself from his cradle, and I believe that the effect would be astonishing. Even now, the German workman, with 20, 30, or 40 per cent. lower wages and far less leisure, appears to be as well off as the Englishman. Always expecting the rainy day, he scrapes to prepare for it; the Englishman, as a rule, does not expect it, and does not prepare. The German does not live so luxuriously; consequently, when reduced to shorter allowance, he can endure it better; he can bear the fall, because he never rises so high. There are no beggars in the streets, no vagrants tramping from town to town as we see them here, and few, if any, hereditary paupers in the workhouses. Education has made the German far seeing, he "cuts his coat according to his cloth," and makes it wear. He extracts pleasure from books, music, and innocent amusements, and although he is fond of the cheap and comparatively harmless beer of the country, which he drinks in great quantities, he does not get drunk; in fact, I think I have seen more drunken men on an ordinary Saturday night in the streets of Keighley, than in Germany during my three visits put together.

To carry the comparison thus far, and there to stop, would convey an inexact impression of the characteristic features of English, as contrasted with German life and manners. I must endeavour to guard my meaning more closely. It is not institutions alone which make the men of any country what they are, still less their educational institu-

tions taken by themselves. I am indebted to a friend* for a comparison of the influences which have determined to a great extent the different characteristics of Germans and Englishmen, which even at the risk of a digression I will quote, as it is of a very instructive character. He says:—
" Among many conditions which determine national character three are specially influential—stock or race, history, and existing institutions. Of race-characters, which are, perhaps, the most important of the three, we need say nothing, for the Germans and ourselves have the same Teutonic ancestry. But the national histories of the two countries, and those second instincts which are bred in men by the course of public events during many generations, have worked very different results in England and Germany. There we read incessantly of invasions, of plunder, of dynastic wars, of family rights pursued to the ruin of nations. We find Frankish, Saxon, Franconian, Swabian, Austrian, and French Emperors. We find kingdoms, like Saxony, divided and parcelled out every few years afresh, so as never to be recognisable for a century together. We find tracts of land, as on the banks of the Rhine, which are by turns German, French, and independent. We find wars of succession without end. We find a Thirty Years' War, perhaps the most terrible thing of its kind known; while the deadliest campaigns of Louis XIV., Marlborough, Frederick the Great, the Revolutionary Armies and Napoleon, were carried out on German ground. Family feuds, rights of succession, pragmatic sanctions made up the public history of the time. Meanwhile the real life of Germany was stifled. From the time when it found full expression, in Northern Germany at least, at the Reformation, down

---

* Mr. L. C. Miall.

to our own age, it seems to have been hidden and well nigh extinct. Literature and art sank so low that in two whole centuries we can name no poet, no historian, no painter, no architect, whose name is known throughout Europe.

" England, cut off by sea from her neighbours, has had a happier fate. We, too, have gone through our revolutions and our struggles, but we have been free from effective foreign invasion for six centuries and a-half, and our continental wars have in most cases meant restlessness rather than desperation. We have held to the old Teutonic rule by King, Council of Nobles, and Assembly of the People. Our national life has been continuous, our development—whether healthy for the time or not—has been spontaneous. We have been free to work out our own thoughts in history, philosophy, and in the fine arts. We have been left undisturbed to construct our industrial system.

" These historical facts explain some at least of the striking differences between Englishmen and Germans. We can see how the German has come to be enduring, submissive, attached to all which increases coherence and unity, while the Englishman is sturdy, obstinate, and independent. We can understand the more cosmopolitan character of the German mind, its disposition to seek light from any quarter, and its capacity for far-reaching thought. We can, in part, account for the provincial flavour of the Englishman's mind, and his honest faith in things English.

" Race and past history we cannot control; and, if we would modify the character of a people, we can only hope to reach it through their institutions. It was a great and wise thought of the Prussian statesman, Stein, when he saw his country humbled into the dust by the battle of Jena, that the restoration of Germany must be mainly effected by her schools. Prussia owes to him, more than to anyone else, her present educational system, her military strength, and her political unity. To the care which Germans have bestowed upon their schools are unquestionably due the banishment of utter ignorance from German soil ; in part, also, the capacity for intelligent obedience, which Germans possess beyond other nations, and the love of harmless and cultivated recreation. The Germans themselves are strong in the belief that the national morality has been mended by education. There are things greater than these—manliness, love of freedom, religious sincerity; and here, as Englishmen, we may fairly claim some degree of superiority.

"In trying to reform our institutions it is more necessary to regard our defects than our excellencies. What a long course of political freedom and independent life can effect has been done for our national character, and we need not learn from Germans what liberty in thought and action means. But Germany has beaten us thoroughly in culture and in provision for the intellectual wants of the very poorest. Let us be thankful in silence for our advantages, feeling how little any voluntary effort of ours has done to secure them. Let us be willing to learn from others how to strengthen our weak points. Happily for us, our deficiencies, though serious, are remediable, and the lessons we have to learn are more easily taught than some others."

I make this quotation with pleasure, because it expresses so clearly my own opinions, and will qualify any possible impression I may have given that Germans and German institutions are, as such, better than the men and institutions of England. It is not my province to balance the purer domestic life of England by the greater public decency of Germany, to set off our independence against their docility,

F

our individuality against their orderliness. For the present purpose it is sufficient that that we have to concede to superior excellence of their schools; the Germans know better than we how to teach the boy and girl of ten and the young man of twenty.

To sum up what I have to say under this head, England is unquestionably behind other nations in the education of her people. We are behind America, Belgium, Holland, Germany, and Switzerland. An Education Bill has at length been passed, and its enlightened administration will to a great extent remove the stain of ignorance which now disgraces the great mass of the English people. But a national education offering to every class in the country the highest requisite training for their duties in life, and letting down the ladder of learning from the universities and science colleges to the elementary schools, so that the deserving poor boy or girl could climb to the top, would more than anything else change the face of English society.

Before, however, this can be done, our educational system must be reformed beyond anything that Acts of Parliament have yet done for us. Mr. Forster's Bill has had the effect of opening the eyes of the nation to the importance of this question, and practical results of no mean character have been achieved, but the work of the statesman will not be completed until the following conditions are satisfied :—

1. A sound elementary education must be placed within the reach of every child in the country. This must be done, not after the manner of the permissive measure of 1870, leaving each locality, whether Denominationalist, Voluntaryist, or Nationalist, to decide for itself whether there shall be schools, what sort of schools, and whether children shall be compelled to attend them; but on a consistent

principle, with a guarantee that the child of the poor man, whether his school be situated in the agricultural districts of Dorset or Devonshire, or in the thriving manufacturing towns of Yorkshire or Lancashire, shall be educated efficiently and under one comprehensive system. In the little State of Saxony, previously alluded to, a child leaving one district and going to another is able to enter a school near his new home, join a class identical with the one he has left, learn from the same books and by the same method, without any drawback whatever ; and you may be sure that whatever can be done in Saxony can be done in England.

2. The Endowed Schools Act of 1869 has done much to reform our Secondary Education, but great extension is required before every town possesses its efficient and appropriate public secondary school. Existing endowments should, of course, be fully utilised, and where endowments are not provided, the State and municipality might be invoked to supply their share of funds ; but in every town—or group of villages—there should be secondary schools suited to the wants of the locality, providing the training needed respectively by professional men and men of business ; and these schools should be linked to the elementary schools, so as to become natural stepping-stones to something higher.

Fresh legislative powers are needed to inaugurate a system adapted to all cases. Recognising the principle that each district will ultimately be the best judge of its own wants, I hope to see the organisation of secondary, as well as of primary instruction, placed in the hands of managers appointed, in part at least, by the municipality.

3. Secondary schools of an equally efficient character should be provided for girls also.

4. Industrial, Science, and Art schools connected with Mechanics' Institutes or otherwise, but so arranged as to afford full opportunity for the attendance of artisans and others actually engaged in trades and manufactures, should be established in every manufacturing town.

5. The universities should be fully utilised as part of the national system, and provide professional and literary education of the highest kind.

6. Scientific colleges of the highest grade should be united with the last mentioned, or established independently in convenient centres.

Some such scheme as this, I believe, would generally be recognised by educationists as requisite to a thoroughly national system of education. The discussion of its practicability, and of the means of realising it, involves the answer to the question previously put :—" How the education of the boys and girls of Keighley may be made more systematic, comprehensive, and general ?"

This is a practical question, and every day increases the urgency with which it demands settlement. At this moment its importance is recognised by all parties in the town, and yet its practical solution is evaded in a most unaccountable manner. Many well-disposed persons readily say, " We are well off as we are, had we not better let *well* alone ?" In the meantime many children are growing up who do not attend school, and already, according to official returns, there is a deficiency of accommodation for some hundreds. Although the comparison between Keighley and other places, as the District School Inspector put the matter forcibly to me the other day, "might not be unfavourable to Keighley at present, yet as most other important places are pushing forward in the cause of education, they will in a couple of years leave Keighley far behind." Opinions of this character from such an authoritative source cannot be put aside; and, further than this, we ought not to rest content with a system of education which practically turns out into the world 70 or 80 per cent. of the scholars unable to pass a simple examination in reading, writing, and arithmetic. Calculated by any method adopted in the ordinary transactions of trade, where, in the manufacture of articles, the cost of the "wasters" is added to the cost of producing those which "pass," our English schools (and with them the Keighley schools) are amongst the most costly in the world, because they have least educational results to show for the money spent.

It is in the power of the people of Keighley to deal with this question and to change this state of things effectually, quietly and economically, so as to bring about a most wonderful improvement, and establish an educational scheme which might even be accepted as a model for an industrial town by the country at large. To attain these results—

1. We must improve the elementary schools of the town, and render the teaching much more efficient than it has been in the past; we must provide accommodation of the most approved character for the several hundreds of children for whom there is not accommodation at present; include in the school course the rudiments of science and drawing; establish a communication with public secondary schools; and *enforce the attendance of all children of school age. These requirements imply the immediate election of a School Board.*

2. I have already dwelt upon the want of good secondary schools in many parts of the country. Keighley is better off in this respect than most of its neighbours, and our secondary education appears to me to require extension rather than

reform. The recently established Trade School* may be made capable of supplying the wants of those who require a practical or scientific education. Through the instrumentality of state grants upon the success of artisans in science and art, it is highly probable that the advantages offered to pupils of that class, of entering the school at half-fees, will be continued. In view of the growth and importance of the town, larger provision may be required for those desirous of receiving a more complete classical training. The founding of scholarships by the Endowed Schools Commissioners, by means of which, a certain number of pupils from elementary schools are yearly admitted to the Trade School, free of charge, has enabled the two classes of schools to work harmoniously together, as I trust they will continue to do with benefit to both. The Trade School supplies an education almost identical with that of the Real or Practical Schools of North Germany.

The reorganised Grammar School will be able to supply for girls a secondary education of a suitable character.

Just as it is of the utmost importance that the greatest possible facilities should be offered of passing from the lower to these higher schools, so it is equally desirable that means should be afforded of advancing beyond these to colleges or universities.

3. The question of providing secondary and scientific education for those boys and young men who can only receive it in evening classes is of the utmost importance to a manufacturing town such as Keighley, where of necessity boys leave school at a comparatively early age, and afterwards enjoy a fair amount of leisure. We cannot expect

---

* See "An Educational Experiment in Yorkshire."—*Blackwood's Magazine*, February, 1872.

for some time at least that any important changes will be
made in the government system of assisting Science and Art
by payment on results, although by giving a better guarantee
of the permanency of state grants the career of science
teachers would be more worthy of ambition, and would
probably be taken up by men of higher qualifications than
those possessed by many teachers at present. In the absence
of more appropriate means the resources of our Mechanics'
Institute and Schools of Science and Art seem to be ample
for supplying present wants, and may be made capable of
keeping pace with the requirements of the future. The
success of the Institute also proves that the all-important
subject of technical education may be pursued by the artisan
and manufacturer with wonderful advantage in the evening
classes, and past experience gives encouragement that under
more systematic and complete elementary instruction these
classes might supply the place of such technical schools
as have so much developed the industries of the continent
during the past twenty years.

4. To pass beyond the secondary day or night school
is at present almost impossible to the artisan, and difficult
to all but the wealthy. The scholarships of the Science
and Art Department, and those founded by Sir Joseph
Whitworth will do something, but they are not numerous,
and can only be won by men of brilliant parts and high
attainments.

There are not a few in this great and wealthy county who
hope to see an efficient scientific college provided in our
midst. Could we follow the noble example of Newcastle
there might be a Polytechnic School for the West Riding,
adequately equipped for teaching pure and applied science,
holding out a helping hand to the promising students in our

town schools, and sending out, year by year, a number of trained men to work in our mines, forges, mills, and schools. The want is even now urgent, and surely here if anywhere, funds will not be refused when a well contrived scheme is earnestly put forth. Whatever may be the fate of the project now, and for a long time, before the public, we must speedily set ourselves to undertake the work in some shape or other.

Such, in my opinion, are the educational requirements of the town of Keighley, and by making the most of the means within our reach—so far as those means do not obstruct a sound plan of progression—we shall most effectually deal with the mass of ignorance that impedes the moral and social advancement of our community.

In bringing forward the facts which I have so imperfectly presented to you, I have no selfish purpose to serve, neither do I wish to wound the feelings of any individual. Mr. Forster, in one of his speeches, well said, "I am not one of those who say that knowledge is virtue ; but I do say this, that ignorance is weakness, and that it is weakness to resist temptation that fills your prisons, and weakness to carry on the struggle of life that fills your workhouses." And whether the question be regarded as a local or a national one, I am most truly convinced, that in a small country like this, where we have to depend for our position; nay our very existence, upon the units of our population, it is of vital importance that every man and woman should be made of the greatest possible value as citizens of a great nation, and to attain this it is our duty, whatever difficulties stand in the way, to lead their human souls to what is best, so as to make what is best out of them. "These two objects are always attainable together, and by the same means," for "the training which makes men happiest in themselves, also makes them most serviceable to others." This, says one of our most thoughtful writers, is the aim of education, and the share of the work which our schools have to do, should be done thoroughly and well. But if education be good for one member of the state it is good for all, and as a matter of political safety, of morals, and of usefulness, every child in the kingdom ought to be educated.

And we all know that England cannot afford to be permanently behind any other nation or country in a great and good thing. In material things we have never hesitated to revolutionise our most expensive processes of manufacture, if advantage could be seen to accrue from the change. We never have been far behind in taking up any commercial project, if only it would pay. Time was, when in this district, organised mobs sought to break to pieces power looms, or burn down factories, because they feared that machinery would cause their ruin. Yet in spite of all, the use of machinery goes on developing our industry ; and there is no machine that will increase production, or facilitate or dispense with manual labour, that is not seized, perfected, and made the most of. There is no engine of destruction invented in the arts of war that England does not procure and manufacture at any cost. Millions and millions have been spent without a murmur in remodelling our navy, because there appeared to be a danger that it would be weaker than the other navies of the world combined. We have been spending millions upon improving our army and "means of defence." For years we have been investing our capital in developing our commerce, while till lately the multitude of the people—in spite of all our talk and boasting—has been lying at our feet neglected. "And the great cry that rises from all our manufacturing cities, louder than their furnace blast, is all in very deed for this—that we manufacture everything there except men; we blanch cotton and strengthen steel, and refine sugar and shape pottery; but to brighten, to strengthen, to refine, or to form a single living spirit never enters into our estimate of advantages."* And when the time comes that man shall be developed as a man and not as a machine, he will be proportionally elevated as a man; and, as the mind governs the hand, so his intelligence will direct his labour into new fields and profitable channels, and make him more valuable to himself and a source of greater strength to the nation.

It will never do for us at Keighley to remain as we are while others are marching on. Education but participates in the general movement.

The old order changeth, yielding place to new.

Our wooden ships were invincible so long as other ships were wooden; the long bow was capable of doing good service while only the long bow was opposed to it; but what can wooden ships and long bows do against ironclads and needleguns? And how will the elementary schools of to-days stand in relation to the national schools of the future? The stage coaches of England were useful conveyances in their day, and afforded rapid means of communication as compared with any others then existing, but we did not on that account refuse to support railways. There were many "interests" that opposed railways, and some influential corporations and wealthy landowners kept them as far as possible from their towns, and went on building coaches in order to compete with them. Many, however, of these corporations and landowners have since seen the folly of their ways, and they have been

---

* Ruskin's Stones of Venice, Vol. 2, page 165.

glad to give to the railway system their hearty support. But the old spirit has not by any means died out, and even the Education Act is most stoutly resisted by those whose "existing interests" it has been so carefully designed to protect. With all its shortcomings, however, it has achieved the great result, which I believe Mr. Forster had in view when he framed it. It has placed the education of the people in the hands of the people. And we may rely upon this —here I quote the words of Mr. Matthew Arnold—"that the moment the working classes of this country have this question of instruction really brought home to them, their self-respect will make them demand, like the working classes on the continent, *public* schools, and not schools which the clergyman, squire, or millowner calls ' my school.' " Denominationalism has done much in providing the present modicum of elementary instruction possessed by this country, but by its opposition to the formation of school boards it is now in danger of impeding the very movement, which I admit it has been so anxious to promote.

I have said this much under a consciousness of many disqualifications. I know that my knowledge is defective on important points. It may be that I am unconsciously biassed this way or that; that I have not fairly communicated my meaning. I can only ask you to search into the matter for yourselves, and see if this be so. When the people of England undertake an inquiry they will, I am confident, come to just conclusions, whether similar to those here set forth or not. Only one thing I would deprecate most strenuously, and that is apathy. When we neglect the Education question—refuse to learn our position, refuse to consider how it may be amended — then, most assuredly, we cannot but be wrong.

We speak of the maintenance of our educational position among the nations as a competition, a race, or a fight. Perhaps it would be wiser to regard it simply as a piece of work—necessary, laborious, and enduring. To do this work faithfully means knowledge for the people, bringing with it comfort, contentment, and improved morality. To neglect it means wide-spread ignorance, and with that are bound up pauperism and crime. Let us make our choice and maintain it.

WM. BYLES AND SON, PRINTERS, BRADFORD.